CW01649881

To [illegible] s
who appre[illegible]
the honesty of
the poet and
the fighters!
Shalom,
Aviva
Kempner
11/25/86

# MY LITTLE SISTER
# AND SELECTED POEMS 1965–1985

FIELD TRANSLATION SERIES 11

Abba Kovner

# MY LITTLE SISTER

## AND SELECTED POEMS 1965-1985

Selected and translated
by Shirley Kaufman

FIELD Translation Series 11

Publication of this book was made possible through a grant from the Ohio Arts Council.

Copyright © 1986 by Oberlin College

Library of Congress Cataloging in Publication Data
Kovner, Abba (Translated by Shirley Kaufman)
MY LITTLE SISTER AND SELECTED POEMS
1965–1985
(The FIELD Translation Series; v. 11)

LC: 85–073146

ISBN: 0–932440–20–7
0–932440–21–5 (paperback)

"It is enough for the poet to be the guilty conscience of his time."

— St. John Perse

"Past and present and future are not disjoin'd but join'd. The greatest poet forms the consistence of what is to be, from what has been and is. He drags the dead out of their coffins and stands them again on their feet. He says to the past, 'Rise and walk before me that I may realize you.' "

— Walt Whitman

CONTENTS

## ACKNOWLEDGMENTS

My gratitude begins with Nurit Orchan who introduced me to the poetry of Abba Kovner when she came to San Francisco from Kibbutz Ein Hahoresh, and has continued to translate his work with me in Jerusalem. Thanks also to Robert Alter and T. Carmi who consulted with me and with the poet on the first version of the translation of *My Little Sister*, and to Ruth Adler for her help with *A Canopy in the Desert*. Judith Levy and Shlomith Rimmon gave me valuable assistance when I first came to live in Jerusalem, and Dan Laor, especially in the more recent poems. I am particularly indebted to Chana Bloch and my husband, H. M. Daleski, for their suggestions and perceptive reading of this entire manuscript. And to Abba Kovner himself, who has participated in these translations from the beginning.

Some of these translations first appeared in *Ariel, Field, The Jerusalem Quarterly, Midstream, Pequod, Poet Lore, Tri-Quarterly*, and in the following anthologies: *New Writing from Israel*, ed. by Jacob Sontag, Corgi Books, London, 1976; *Fourteen Israeli*

*Poets*, ed. by Dennis Silk, Andre Deutsch, London, 1976; *New Writing in Israel*, ed. by Ezra Spicehandler, Schocken Books, N.Y., and Sabra Books, Tel Aviv, 1976; *Contemporary Israeli Literature*, ed. by Elliott Anderson, Jewish Publication Society, Philadelphia, 1977; *Voices from the Ark*, ed. by Howard Schwartz and Anthony Rudolf, Avon Books, 1980; *Literature from the World*, ed. by Warren Carrier and Bonnie Newman, Charles Scribner's Sons, N.Y., 1981; and *45 Contemporary Poems*, ed. by Alberta Turner, Longman, Inc., 1985.

An earlier version of *My Little Sister* was originally published in *Abba Kovner and Nelly Sachs: Selected Poems*, in the Penguin Modern European Poets series, Penguin Books, Harmondsworth, England, 1971, and reprinted in *A Canopy in the Desert: Selected Poems*, together with the complete poem of that title and earlier versions of some of the poems from *From All the Loves*, by the University of Pittsburgh Press, 1973, © Shirley Kaufman.

*From All the Loves* was originally published in Hebrew under the title, *Mikol Haahavot* (Tel Aviv: Sifriat Poalim, 1965).

*My Little Sister* was originally published in Hebrew under the title, *Ahoti Ktana* (Tel Aviv: Sifriat Poalim, 1967).

*A Canopy in the Desert* was originally published in Hebrew under the title, *Hupa Bamidbar* (Tel Aviv: Sifriat Poalim, 1970.

The above books copyright © Abba Kovner and Sifriat Poalim, 1970.

*Observations* was originally published in Hebrew under the title *Tatzpiot* (Tel Aviv: Sifriat Poalim, 1977)

*To* was originally published in Hebrew under the title *El* (Tel Aviv: © Abba Kovner and Hakibbutz Hameuhad, 1980).

# INTRODUCTION

A cloister's wall is high.
A wall of silence
still higher.

*My Little Sister*, 8

"During the trial of Adolph Eichmann," Abba Kovner recalls, "I tried to make clear the special feeling of isolation common to European Jews. In answer to a question from one of the judges, I explained that there were three walls of isolation. The first wall was a physical wall that the Germans put up between us and the world. If you tore this wall down there was another one — the neighbors you lived with before the war, who had become a threatening wall. And behind this there was a third wall — a feeling that the whole world outside was indifferent."

Testimony in a courtroom is one thing, but the transformation of such feeling, memory, and experience into art is something quite different.

Abba Kovner has asked how "a literary gesture could be enough to bear testimony to the depths of the suffering contained in the word 'ghetto.' " The ghettos in Nazi Europe and the death camps to which they led, like Auschwitz, have no parallel in anything that has happened to human beings anywhere in the world, before or since. Millions were slain in the Stalin purges, starved in Mao's famine, brutally murdered in Uganda and Kampuchea, but the Nazi Holocaust remains the archetype of man's inhumanity to man. The fact that a civilized Western nation conceived the outrage of genocide and executed the plan with technological precision over a period of years while the rest of the world looked the other way, is still beyond comprehension. The collective Jewish agony in the days of the "final solution" cannot be described in words like "slaughter" or "massacre" or "holocaust." Kovner's work, however, is not a literary gesture. It is a cry, powerfully muted, from the depths of a man who resisted that bestial and perfectly mechanized genocide of six million and who survived. Kovner is one of the few, like Paul Celan and Nelly Sachs, who have been able to transmute such an experience into poems that can change our lives.

"Despair and hope, sacrifice and promise, exist side by side in Jewish history, each equally real, irreconcilable opposites. . . . Abba Kovner seeks and discovers metaphysical significance in suffering," wrote Stephen Spender in his introduction to Kovner's *My Little Sister* when it was first published by Penguin in 1971 with a selection of poems by Nelly Sachs. Spender asked "whether the threat of universal catastrophe today is not beginning to produce a world consciousness more communal than individualist, and whether this may not produce a poetry closer in attitude to that of the Jewish poets (Kovner and Sachs) than to that of the great individualist poets who were writing in America and England early in the present century."

Actual confrontation, rather than threat, has formed the consciousness of poets like Kovner, who said in a recent interview:

> Perhaps this explains why Hebrew poetry remains so different, whether we like it or not, from any other poetry. Because even when you

— the poet — put the entire world in parenthesis and speak only to yourself, only with your personal "I," you are in fact participating in a communal prayer. This is a burden almost unbearable.

*

Abba Kovner was born in 1918 in the Crimea where his family had gone from a town near Vilna, Lithuania, on their way to Palestine. They were caught in Sevastopol, unable to leave, when World War I broke out, and settled in Vilna after the war. In 1941 the Germans established the ghetto in Vilna. They had already occupied a strip of Russian territory from the Baltic to the Black Sea, a strip behind which six million Jews were trapped. From June to November the Nazis took more than 40,000 Jews out of Vilna. They said they were taking them to a labor camp at Ponar; the rest, who were locked behind the gates of the ghetto, would go when the camp and its factories could absorb them. A Dominican convent in the area volunteered to hide some young people who otherwise would have been taken "to work" by the Nazis. Kovner hid in this convent for three months, dressed as a nun, sometimes working in the fields with the Mother Superior. (It was twenty years before he could transform this experience in *My Little Sister.*) A priest who came to say Mass for the nuns told him what he had observed around Ponar, that Jews were brought there in trucks and horse-drawn carts, and the trucks and carts came back empty, and that there was no apparent logic to the "selections" by the Germans. With a growing certainty that all the Jews of Europe were to be destroyed and that the Jews of Vilna were only the first in line, Kovner left the safety of the convent and returned to the ghetto.

In November 1941 a young girl crawled up over the butchered bodies in the pits at Ponar and made her way eight miles through a frozen forest back to the Vilna ghetto. No one could believe her story — thousands of Jews lined up, shot, and piled in a ditch. But Abba Kovner listened to her. He was twenty-two years old. He had already lost his first love at Ponar and would soon lose his mother. He wrote the first Jewish call to arms in the Vilna ghetto, a pathetic call since the Jews there had no arms or ammunition. But as he later said, "in a situation where there is no hope, fighting creates a sort of hope."

In the coming months the 70,000 Jews of Vilna, like the Jews in other ghettos in Eastern Europe, starved, diseased, terrorized by incredible savagery, saw nothing ahead but death and madness. Abba Kovner became the leader of their fighting resistance, the United Partisan Organization. He and a few others began to take whoever could walk or crawl out of the ghetto through the sewers into the forests. Only a few hundred survived. It is not surprising that such an experience would shape the rest of Kovner's life and become the main subject of his poetry, even forty years later.

After the war, Kovner organized the first group of the *Bricha* movement, the flight of refugee Jews to Palestine. They travelled from all parts of Europe to ports in Italy and embarked for Palestine in 1945. Kovner was arrested by the British and imprisoned in Cairo before he was finally transferred to a Jerusalem prison from which the Haganah (Jewish underground army before the State) succeeded in freeing him. This is how Kovner describes his arrival in Palestine:

> I had come through the Suez Canal and Sinai, or rather, I was brought, handcuffed, in a military

command car. I remember a long, exhausting journey that numbed all the senses . . . how I was stunned and dazzled by the light . . . I couldn't look ahead all the time at the mountains and the sky, so I looked at the ground, at the wheels of the command car. Less than a year earlier I had seen a different earth running beneath me. On the way from Budapest to Vienna from the roof of an express train. I lay on the roof of that train in order to cross the border illegally. Hanging on tight, my face to the ground, I had watched how the ground seemed to be running away from me, fleeing like a panic-stricken herd of animals. Here, too, the earth was running, but this time it was running toward me, like a wave coming into my arms.

from *On the Narrow Bridge*, p. 160
(Tel Aviv: Sifriat Poalim, 1981)

Even when he writes about his life in Israel, Kovner never forgets what happened in Europe. But the past is not recreated for its own sake. It has become part of the present, as in "And There You Were," where the dead ghetto fighter joins the living as they watch a TV documentary, or in "Changing the Order," with its very domestic details of kibbutz life. Kovner became a member of Kibbutz Ein Hahoresh soon after his arrival. He still lives there with his wife, Vitka, who is also well-known for her heroism as a partisan. During the Israeli War of Independence in 1948 he served on the southern front.

His work includes a novel about the War of Independence; several collections he has edited of writings by partisans, Holocaust survivors, and Israeli children living in border settlements at the time of the Six Day War; essays and speeches recently collected in a book titled *On the Narrow Bridge*; and ten volumes of poetry, six of them lyric-dramatic book-length poems which bring together personal and historical material. *My Little Sister*, Kovner's major poem sequence, appears here in a newly revised translation, with a selection of poems written since 1965, chosen with the aim of collecting in English Kovner's most representative work.

*

Biblical allusions are often lost when they appear out of context in a language other than the original Hebrew. When Kovner writes in *My Little Sister*, "*ahoti kala*" ("my sister, my spouse"), the words echo like music from the Song of Songs (4:9–12 and 5:1). Throughout the sequence there are phrases juxtaposing the beloved sister-bride of the Song of Songs with the Holocaust sister whose bridegroom will never bring her "into his chambers" (*My Little Sister*, 29; Song of Songs 1:4). And in the poem "Falling Rocks," to cite another example, the end of section 22 comes from the Hebrew of Exodus 14:21, and becomes a dream of wish-fulfillment, the sea opening for the Holocaust victims as the Red Sea opened for Moses when he led his people out of slavery in Egypt. One must be alert to these allusions in Kovner's poetry on almost every page.

In many passages Kovner continues the ancient tradition of the *piyut* or liturgical poem, most notably in *My Little Sister*, 41. The original *piyut* was a metrical composition inspired by synagogue services. This prayer-poem borrowed its language from the biblical commentaries on the Midrash and Talmud (as in the poem "Drowned"). The sounds played an important part in turning the mind of the reader to the deeper meanings. Kovner also likes to use graphic techniques, often arranging words for emphasis in columns or in upside-down pyramids. His skill in Hebrew — the effects he creates by rhyme, assonance, unusual syntax, dramatic shifts in diction — is formidable, and can only be approximated in English.

If we do not know the Bible, and the words cannot resound for us in the original context, if we do not know all the details of Kovner's own life, so that we cannot use these private experiences to enlarge our understanding of his historical and personal poems, the poetry still speaks to us. For Kovner's language and symbolism are not exclusively private. *Ashes, walls, hopeless wars, mushroom cloud*, and *lost children* belong to a world we recognize, from the Nazi death camps to Hiroshima to Vietnam. Kovner's experience is strongly personal, but our perception of it makes it universal.

Kovner speaks in what T. S. Eliot has called "the three voices of poetry." We hear the voice of the poet talking to himself, talking to us, and talking through the characters he creates. Frequently he shifts the voices. The poet switches from first to second to third person. We, you, I, she — they all become one. And these voices transcend the limits of time. They speak from the ancient past, the immediate yesterday, even the future.

*

"Poetry," says Kovner, "is, in a sense, a request for pardon for what we do in our lives, and for what was done to us. If there is any moral meaning to poetry in general, perhaps this is it. A way of asking forgiveness for the evil in human existence."

Kovner has seen the apotheosis of evil in the Nazis' genocidal crimes. He has lived with the horror of people being shoveled into mass graves (including his own family), gassed, and burned alive; of the free nations of the world doing nothing about rescue; of the sinking of shiploads of survivors in the waters of the Mediterranean because the British would not let them enter Palestine and because no other country would take them. He has also seen the rebirth of his national homeland in the State of Israel, a return to life out of the ashes of Europe. The image that seems to focus all this for Kovner is his confrontation with the half-dead, half-crazed girl (the sister he never had, the love who never came back) from the mass grave at Ponar. Her face haunts every line he writes. She appears in poem after poem as *daughter, sister, my love, you*, never by name. We do not see her features. Her eyes are ashes. But we hear her voice. And the silence after the voice.

Shirley Kaufman
January, 1986
Jerusalem, Israel

## from
## FROM ALL THE LOVES

(*Mikol Ha-ahavot*)
1965

. . . my hands will never
touch you. Your coffin
never leave my shoulders.

## THEY BUILD HOUSES IN EIN HAHORESH

They build houses in Ein Hahoresh just like the
rest of the world.
First they lay a foundation,
they add walls, and finally
they pour the reinforced concrete roof.
Maybe it's crazy, but I'll try
with my own hands, maybe
in my last years,
to build another house. First I'll pour concrete
the size of my body, without doors.
I'll install a window
(why do they leave the windows for the end?)
and if I don't have a big enough foundation
for my head,
I'll call through the window
to you, my love.

## WHAT'S NOT IN THE HEART

1

I do not hold a mirage in my hand —
my shirt's in my hand. The plain filled
with my wheat. All of it. Soaked by dew
flat at my feet. Its beauty
turns each image pale. The returning heron
and the apple garden. Sun
plucks at my shoulders like my daughter's
    fingers.
And this day
recalling soon
the smell of the harvest:
this morning (I say to myself)
even in the burned forest the bird
has come back to sing.

2

Useless. I try now to understand that what
        happened
happened. We declared two minutes of silence
so silence would not grow in the windows
of our homes. And no way out, my brother.
The world does not stand on a cry

at night. On a man
with something in his heart, because
what's in the heart is nothing. Because
the living live by the will of those who go
where they were not willing to go.

Useless: I try now to define who you were —
word-shadows! Only your returning shadow
exists. My hands will never
touch you. Your coffin
never leaves my shoulders.

## GIVE A SIGN

Give a sign    a sign    a sign
to the shore. To me. Don't call my name,
kiss the ice floating. Beat at the wall
like a prisoner. As the condemned beats his head.
Like one who goes up to the gallows, built
knowingly
by the defendant
with bare hands
with teeth that bit off the iron bars
he loved. Disgusting to think one could
want American ice cream and you
with the same lips
blessed by a penny. With a river's urge
to return to the mountain. To accept
without stretching your neck to the knife
without a sack of tears
on the back. And to say
let it be. To get used
to autumn.
Yesterday.
Today. Again.

Your closed eyes! I am two steps from you.
Maybe we weren't meant for anything
worthwhile. Of negotiable value.
Maybe we'll only be formed out of scorched
earth. So what. I refuse to die
in friendship.
In bird-down.
In a life of nothing.

## LORD OF HOSTS

### 1

Bulls did not come to the arena to fight
but to mourn. And their eyes, they tell us,
the bulls' eyes are color-blind!
If only that silly rag would touch them,
like lightning, a call of salvation,
their blindness would split the darkness
of arenas and cities. And like fire
in a thick forest, their dumbness would burn
in a final light smashing
the blood                                        my blood

is silent. Flocks of cooing flags
on my roofs. And not one rag.
One rag,
Lord! In exchange for my eyes.

2

Maybe — this too is courage. Maybe
glory in a drained cup of wine.
But it's terrible. So terrible
to wake up in the morning without a dream
to daylight.
Daylight.
A day spread precise as the sleeves
of a white shirt on a clothesline.

3

Your landscape in light. In full light
my hands. In a glass aquarium
a gold fish stares
at me. (Daughter. Daughter. Where did you buy
the gold ribbon for your hair?)
I will come
to turn on the light in your window.

## NEAR

### 1 Abel

Light the candle I will return    to you:  morning
rises and smoke on the face of the deep and I
                                        in the field
alone                                   heaps of feathers
flutter under the sky and I can't              tell
if the birds      dropped them all when they died
                              or the quilt and pillows
when they were torn to shreds (I heard
                                        the wind
hissing) lost their entrails                  outside
at dawn
                    very white feathers whine there
between water and sky          if You have any
mercy put them      my God where the birds are

## 2 Cain

I swore I didn't hear You all day
calling Where are you
it's not You I feared when I escaped
but all the terrible noises I remember a voice
from a shed like broken sounds of the shofar
(my house stood
between stables and eucalyptus)
and her small braided head.
Your day did not open her eyes

Now a continent rises around me perfumed
a guilt offering of incense for the whole world
its innocence shines like the sky's radiance
on the desert of stone the pillar of man
in the image of a mushroom cloud.
Light the candle we will return
to You: morning rises
there's no other
messenger but
You where are
You and
I

## WHEN I FIRST HUNG IT

When I first hung my father's portrait
(in charcoal, black and white)
my heart clapped its hands.
When you put your lips on my mouth
(forever forever forever)
oceans pulled back, my dear.
When Barcelona stood in flames
(oh you who just stood there)
I ran barefoot to Madrid,

and the skies tell how my eyes
avoided yours in the street,
and I don't know how many pennies
you got from the old wretch
for pawning my coat!

It's all neat again. My coat's on my skin.
Father is on the wall. Opposite.
Madrid is white. And you in my tomb.

## DROWNED

He once saw a skull floating on the water's surface. He said to it: because you drowned others, you were drowned . . .

*Ethics of the Fathers* 2:6

*Drowned*
*drowned*
*and finally they themselves will be drowned.*
At the railway station in Hamburg
near the harbor — even today it's there
where it used to be —

in a red hat
he's whistling. The trains come now
into the station of Hamburg every two minutes,
and between the hours

of four and six
in the afternoon there's a river of coming and
 going
loud and constant. The Elbe runs into the sea
and they're on the land and the sea,

and the one who is whistling
whistles like a royal bird in the morning.
And when the express goes out
the commuter train comes in.

And I too saw a skull floating on the water.
The Vilia flows into the Neman, and the Neman
— where does the Neman go?

And I said to my mother, Mother, Berlin
is split in two. My mother said,
My son, what did you name your son?

My wife bore me one. Named for our young
brother, our young unlucky brother.

Now twenty years later my mother smiles —
How was your brother unlucky?

Mother, mother, I reached down to catch
the braids of the water and it wasn't
my mother. Or a woman's skull.

Only a floating slab of the moon.

## EVERYONE WHO COMES

Everyone who comes to the grave of Eliahu, the
Gaon
of Vilna, lies down on the grave and receives
the grace of the Gaon.

The sick — their health again. The barren
woman
fertility, the most impoverished
a scrap of a living.

Many shards in strange shapes
cover the grave of the Gaon,
and many who come here are strange.

And all those who come
are needy. They leave little notes
about what they need.

I wasn't allowed to visit the sacred place.
So I wouldn't know how sorrow cries.
Or maybe I was too young.

Now my friends are amazed
as I prepare for a pilgrimage to his tomb:
I earn my living, my wife has children,

my wounds, they say, are healed. I
lack nothing, nothing
but hope.

## TWO ARE NOT ALWAYS BETTER

Two are not always better than one. A coward
is not always the one who is frightened.
Messengers don't always
rush out at the King's orders.

To kneel.
To kneel
with no good reason no sense
mid-way
in the midst of a storm. To make
paths once more
to the four dunes of heaven.
From a leveled mountain
from a world where nothing remains
not a stone on a stone.
To take a piece of white clay
one handful in order to
shape your smile your eyes
the old wrinkles.
To smooth your small head.

## THE SCIENTISTS ARE WRONG

They're wrong, the scientists. The universe
wasn't created
billions of years ago.
The universe is created every day.

The scientists are wrong to claim
the universe was created from one primordial
substance.
The world is created every day
from various substances with nothing in
common.
Only the relative proportion of their masses,
like the elements of sorrow and hope,
make them companions
and curbstones. I'm sorry

I have to get up, in all modesty, and disagree
with what is so sure and recognized by experts:
that there's no speed faster than the speed of
light,
when I and my lighted flesh
just noticed something else right here —

whose speed is even greater than the speed of
light
and which also returns,
though not in a straight line, because of the
curve of the universe
or because of the innocence of God.

And if we connect all this to an equation,
according to the rules, maybe
it will make sense that I refuse to believe that
her voice
and everything I always cherished
and everything so real and suddenly
lost,
is actually lost forever.

# MY LITTLE SISTER

(*Ahoti Ktana*)

1968

To my children Michael and Shlomit

. . . with what, little sister,
shall we spin and weave the dream
now?

*They came up to a wall.*
*On the seventh night until the dawn*
*heard from the wall the drowning in the snow*
*not seeing the marchers' faces*
*in the white wind.*

## ONE

1

Came up to a wall. The iron ring
of the chime caught in a chunk
of ice. They seized it, rubbed it
like clutching the face of a frozen man.
Until the morning light
with invocations, with weeping nails;
begged the voice of the bell
to break from the frost,
from the killing silence.
And the iron did not shake.
Or tremble.

2

But we were like crazy
dogs gnawing the moon in a puddle.
Then it rang. One
awful ring. How is it
animals and birds inside the wall
did not freeze at the sound!

Nine sainted Sisters
hurried to the gate. Their voices withered.

Naked. Braids on her breast —
my fragile sister!
Standing at the door.

3

My sister's eyes search the wall of the convent
for a scarlet thread. A candle trembles
in the nun's hands.
Nine holy Sisters look at my sister

seeing — ashes that speak.

4

Dawn that wakes from fear. In light
wrenched from smoke, three chestnut trees
appear this morning
as if back from the land of the living.

My sister sees them close by.

My sister does not cry out. Only a catch
of joy in the throat. Nine nuns
are silent in black to my sister
like faces of monuments in a foreign city.

5

The bell rings six.
The Dominican Convent is awake.
The Sisters search my sister's eyes.
My fragile sister!
Nine Sisters look at you
uneasy

seeing — ashes that speak.

6

Angels go with my sister.
A flock of angels goes with my
sister
up to the door. My little sister!
She has taken another god,
a gate opens for her.
And a place.

7

Nine "Little Sisters" in a gold frame
shining with inner light.
Doves ate
from their kissed hands.
When my dove fell down at the foot of the wall,
torn wing,
their palms were folded
in supplication,

pink as prayer beads, joints of their fingers
stiffen,
while my sister stands at the door.

A n d   t h e   s o n   s e e s
A n d   t h e   f a t h e r   s t a r e s

8

A cloister wall is high.
A wall of silence
still higher.

A ladder leans at the side.
Tops of chestnut trees touch and recoil
from the bell tower.
Three chestnut trees
out of a land of lakes

and mud.

9

From here you can see the world
of the living.
From here a whole world watches
my face dissolve into
blue.

My sister is in the wall.
The waylayer at the gates.
In a heavy night robe,
in bare feet,
spying behind her back
god comes near.

10

The place is amazed. What yearning streams
through my land
— that bitch!

These starving eyes
ripe with love.
Silences
and velvet steps.
Such clean hands and pure minds.

From his suffering image,
from the feet of the cold statue,
look, with a delicate hand
dust is swept
into a gold coffer —
only my crucified memory
outside the fence.

In that place,
in a private language, my sister plays
with another god.

11

Walls of the house are bright.

No woman has crouched to give birth
on the floor.
No man screams
blood. Their beds
are made ready with pardons.
Small pardons drop
in the lap
like a whore's pay.
And his light dripping warm.
If you do not come to us
— how can we be consoled?

12

Night after night
the Sisters breathe hard in their beds
as if lifted up on a ladder.
Their bodies tremble.
And this night too, heavy with longing,
the gowns on their skins are burning.

In his high place,
quiet as a tree alone,
he stands.
And light of the mother and the father
trickles down from his face.

Then his bright body breaks out
a gold frame.
Lord! He comes down
on a ladder of thorns.
He does not bleed.

He swings
in his thin limbs.

13

The granter of grace to the innocent
comes.
He arches over me, saying:
you are my daughter —
The sun.
The frost.
The heat.
Together they pierce my flesh.
His blazing forehead on my face
and the great sea in me.
No world but him.
Nothing but him in me.

Only the soul is awake and knows
that this is the lust of knowing.

14

To give to love the
walkers in the snow. The
pressed. The
oppressors. All the
lost for they are lost.
To bring them back
in pity
with open arms
with ringing bells
in blood.

Nine Sisters drenched with pleasure.
Morning rises
for love.
My little sister
is scared.

15

The world that watched
withdrew.
Her beautiful doll,
father's gift,
they crushed in the snow.

No mother, no brother,
hands crossed over her growing breasts,
they waved my sister
through that gate.

Hid her behind the wall.
With sainted patience
the ladies wait.
They are flooded with mercy.

My fragile sister!
No harbor — betrayal
— no island.
Only a folded sail in a storm.

## TWO

### 16

There, just there
a city lies. Body still warm.
Bells are ringing.

17

You have not seen a city thrust on its back
like a horse in its blood, jerking its hooves
unable to rise.

Bells are ringing.

City.
City.
How mourn a city
whose people are dead, whose dead are alive
in the heart.

Bells.

Now the Sisters are ready.
Ringing,
the bells chime their longing
to fixed portions,
to times appointed
for payment. And the wall keeps them
from the world.
Nine little Sisters pace in awe.
Their robes float. In procession.

My sister sits at the window. She
waits for a brother.

18

i

You never knew Vilk. He takes me
in his paws. He wets my eyes
with his warm tongue,
and when he says good night like this,
I hear my father's sandals
going to his room.

Tomorrow Vilk will carry me in his teeth,
and I will be like one of the whelps.

ii

One
bell for prayer.
A second
for danger.

A long rope hangs from one.

My sister's life
from the second.

Free of god,
the dog listens for the hidden bell
at the gate of the convent —
day and night.

iii

He never barks.
Before an alarm
he only bares his teeth.
His eyes are filled with blood.

Then Vilk sets this creature gently
in the secrecy of the kennel. He covers her face
with his hairy body,
stands over her trembling. Mute.

When he was murdered, my sister washed Vilk
from head to foot
and wrote: my brother,
in the sand.

19

Christina is lame. Her day begins
with a murmur of eyelashes. Like a dove
    alarmed from its nest.
Christina circles his face,
a loose wing pleading.
Christina hazards her life waiting
for him to take her to himself.

Christina knows there are endless ways,
but only one
she can choose.
Christina knows fulfillment
is promised,
the gates of heaven in reach of her prayer.

A life for our Sister Christina —
but no perfect healing.

20

The second Christina (they have one God
but not one father) is a red-fleshed
virgin, an excellent mare.
But the way she looks!

Her stricken look when the sun is shining.
And something almost,
not quite love
comes hot,
comes cold.
She labors to sleep,
our Sister Christina. All day long
in rage she drives the little Sisters —
all day long
the virgin kneels.

21

Suzanne is alien. If not to the mother of god,
then to herself.
When there's a tolling to prayer
from the tower,
her head flinches
as from a whip.

22

No!
Don't imagine
a lovelier one than Marie.
My God —

Oh God, keep
far away
the steps of my prince!

23

Irena and Olga are glorious with love.
When they sink down
together
to kiss his thin body,
rinse
his mute face with warm
tears,
my sister's frozen eyes
say:
Blessed are the crucified.
But for whom?

24

Our hearts invented a place,
yes, a place in the world
where we would know life without end.
Your lives, how they seize the future!
To our Sister Clarisse — the world
is a waiting room to be prized.

Blessed the Creator. He has
in His world: such a Sister,
such patience,
such waiting rooms.

25

Most blessed of the nuns the holy flesh
already hallowed by sin.
In order of importance,
she is the clapper of the convent.
Not by her loud voice,
but by her great legs
dragging the mystery of the world.

She knows it. In her lips —
scorched straps — it is chained,
unraveled as a clothesline.
The holy flesh, our Sister.
With head thrust forward she is the first
who marches to confession
like a battering ram to a wall.
A statue could be made
from the stuff in her. With a drawn sword.

She
pities my sister.
And does not like
black sheep.

## THREE

26

My sister loves the Mother Superior.
A hood covers her clear forehead,
not her shivering heart.

My sister sees the Mother Superior.
Maybe her heart trembles with too much fervor.
Maybe she also has no
place to escape.

When the sun couples with the invaders,
the Mother's eyes
keep guarding spring;

when she faces the divine image
in her small

thin shape — his cross falls:
body to body they are
silent. Except for their eyes.
Maybe at the end of time we'll know who's to
blame
that now such a heart
is split!
Every day the Mother Superior drills hymns
into my sister.
She chants to her and does not speak.

My sister sings in another choir.

27

Oh you who commanded us to be children
silent
scared.

The day I turned back
when a black cat crossed my path —

The day I wept for the neighbor's daughter
when her bridegroom found an empty bucket —

Oh night grinding
sleep. Fear entered all my bones
— I cut my nails at the window.

Every Sunday
my window shakes from the bells of St. Mary's,
every Sunday
my heart is dumb with the terror
of drowning —

Oh you who commanded us to be children
more silent than fire.

28

My sister sits happy
at her bridegroom's table. She does not cry.
My sister will do no such thing:
what would people say!

My sister sits happy
at her bridegroom's table. Her heart is awake.
The whole world drinks
kosher chicken soup.

The dumplings of unleavened flour
were made by her mother-in-law. The world
    is amazed
and tastes the mother's dessert.

My sister-bride sits. A small dish
of honey before her. Such a huge crowd!
Father twisted
the braids of the hallah.

Our father took his bread, bless God,
forty years from the same oven. He never
    imagined
a whole people could rise in the ovens
and the world, with God's help, go on.

My sister sits at the table in her bridal veil
alone. From the mourners' hideout
the voice of a bridegroom comes near.
We will set the table without you;
the marriage contract will be written in stone.

29

Oh one who asked for the hand of my sister.
Oh one who closed in on her in the valley
to kiss her on the mouth with no witness.
With lips tasting clay,
my bridegrooms,
go, look for her now.

We put her at the foot of the wall
that understands silence.
We put her on the mound
like a naked stem.
Blessed be he among men
who will bring her into his chambers,
my bridegrooms!

30

White
white
white
in white

the Dominican Convent prays:

God's estate is covered with quiet flowers,
flooded with profound salvation.
What shall we do for our sister
and she like a wilted tendril?

31

A usual morning.
The light of each separate star still
visible.
A bright point of light like an aimless balloon.
My sister
tries to catch

through the lattice.
The light-moth spins off,
the window is frozen.
With a patch of muslin
from the dress of her doll
she stretches her hand for it,
doesn't give up.

32

To watch with soft eyes

the rising morning. Wipe from the lips
the taste of hot ash.
To bring back
the world to innocence,
as if to its socket
a bone from the foot of the dead.
To return there,
to the city,

and plant chestnut trees again
in the square,
common bellflowers
near the fence,
and not to fear,
not to fear that the beating darkness
will suddenly lock up your sobs
in the lines of a poem.

Fragile, my sister!
My fragile sister.

33

In the rustle of chestnuts, in the foaming earth
filled with dark signs,

in the beat of the heart
like a flock of gulls bursting toward you,
in a smell of moss
in the wall,
in joy rising from fissures,
like water collected in cracks,
at the door of your home, my sister,
spring

spring
spring lords over the land!
And dawn opens wide in the valley.
Only your angels are late.
They give no sign.
They won't say when.

Perhaps a rider will return.
Perhaps the brother.
In the woods my sister plays
hopscotch
with the messiah.

34

A tortured forest. Leaves and crown sacrificed

to a violent autumn.
Bare,
against stars of hostile brilliance,
still nurtured tubers of spring.

My home carried its roots
to the stake.
With what —
with what, little sister,
shall we spin and weave the dream
now?

## FOUR

### 35

i

In seventy-seven funerals we circled the wall
and the wall stood.
From the promised land I called you,
I searched for you
among heaps of small shoes.
At every approaching holiday.

No man will cure,
no heaven,
the offense of your scalding silence.

My blessing
did not light your eyes.
My curse
came too late.

ii

— to say good-bye to you
even in one word
whispered
that you were no burden to us.
On the way.
Mother walked heavy.
I.
All your brothers.
And the desperate convoy.
Our strength did not give out,
only the earth, below.

iii

In animal sheds
on cold stoves
when we made our beds
on steaming dung
before eyes wet
with rotten joy
in front of dogs
too proud to bark —

even when shame came into all my limbs
with transparent nails glaring,
we clung to our flesh
as if alive.

Until we lay down
one near the other.
Until we saw our faces
one within the other.
At the edge of the redeeming pit,
my sister,
we remembered your going alone.

36

You were not privileged to be condemned to
 death.
You did not enter a covenant of blood.
On the day when you will be spoken for —
behold you
are consecrated
more than eagles
and angels.

37

I vow by you today.
We will not speak, for better or for worse,
of a ruined world. But terror —
how will this passage of our lives
be told now —

38

This night, just snow.
Follow the dogs,
Put on the dress
our mother sewed for you,

the only one
left, in white folds.

We have no other dress.
We have no other prayer.
This sun,
no other.
Let us rise up, oh sister,
your time has come.

39

Behold you — behold
they . . .
So long as the night covers you like a canopy
let us go forth.
Say to them nicely
thank you.
Be grateful
for every hour
of refuge.
Perhaps they were not guilty —
there is always someone more guilty:
(the victim)
(the victim)

Perhaps they heard
only the voice of their hearts:

Go, they said.
Go.
My fragile sister!
You must
go.
Come, sister,
quiet.
Quiet.

40

We knew what the hazards were —
to cross the soft earth,
to pass the still glowing iron
and to say to a stranger
— a world was here.

It comes upon me from behind
— a choir of stones
here!
In the unrepenting street of the city
the shorn head of my sister
breaks out of a wall.

41

sealed in a tomb
enslaved          troops of scorpions rake me
steal me out, take me          voice of my love
(door)
(door)
house of clay          house of life
undo me          renew me
(door)
(door)
my love a gazelle
who finds me who floods me          who fills me
who sings when I          sorrow
my love who speaks          near now
(over)
(it's over)

## FIVE

42

As when a fire dies. And nobody leaves,
though everything has already
gone out — the flames,
the vault of heaven,
the clothes,
and the brightness
in the eyes of those who stand apart.

The generous will rush together then
to those who were burning. To throw
water
on each of them.
What if a stone's still boiling in their hearts?

43

As in a flood dammed too late,
they will come, come to the shore,
their hearts full of pity, to help
the survivors with swollen feet
into the book of chronicles,

to extend a brother's hand.
And they gave them a hand
in spite of their ugly smell.
And before heart and mind could separate
they cried,
and applauded them.
As in a melodrama that's over:
the *characters*
are asked
to step in front of the curtain.

44

They came out.
They stretched their whole hands for the bread
still fearing hunger.
They stood.
When they smelled plates of soup,
they unwrapped tin spoons
from their leggings.
And all who came near, when they gnawed the
bones,
were like tyrants or thieves.

And they rose up.
In Europe the sun was shining,
and they
bought black umbrellas
as if they were daggers;

and while you stood trembling
I wanted to say to you,
my sister!
Tomorrow they will be first to forget:
they will cover up my blood.

45

The Bikur Holim Hospital
walls soaked
with the smell of sour urine
and dying hopes.

In the old hospital
among walls of red brick
my sister died.

She was two hours old. Suddenly
her eyelids contracted to look —
my sister did not scream.
She was not introduced to the world.

46

You are silent.
But our mother used to light
a candle for the saving of her soul
every day.

The candles ran out in the ghetto, and the
oxygen
in the bunker.
My mother kindled her soul
on all the seas.

Our mother mourned a daughter
who never came into the world.
From 1940 to 1948. The rest of her sons were cut
down,
and she lamented them,
and she mourned my little sister
who never came into the world.

— You who saw
everything.
You who saw us,
mother!
How mourn to our faces
someone
who never came into the world?

And mother stared at me for a while.
And she stared at me for a long while.
Until her lips parted to speak,
and she said, my son
— she was not privileged to see
the light of the day.

And she came close.
And she prepared the candle.
And her hand was holding
another wick.

*no one will carry my mother's bier with me*
*no one will come close to my mother's bier with me*
*come to the vast plains*
*lead your eyes to the white river*
*it scoops out its channel and shoves*
*like the prow of a heavy*
*ship in the ice*
*and say with me*
imi
imi

from

# A CANOPY IN THE DESERT

(*Hupa Bamidbar*)
1970

to Vitka

. . . only you, my little sister, will I take with
me on my back. To carry you beyond
my naked plot of soil.

## EIGHTH GATE:

## A PAUSE AT THE FOOT OF THE MOUNTAIN

Mountain all that preceded
the mountain all that preceded
the mask that preceded
the word
the barrier where
did your footprints disappear?

Proud. My desert is
too proud to answer.

# A DIALOGUE AT NIGHT BY ST. CATHERINE'S MONASTERY A MOUNTAIN BEHIND A MOUNTAIN ABOVE AND RISING THE MOUNTAIN OF MOUNTAINS

A flower is easy to define,
but not light when it rests from its own speed
on the back of an eroded stone. When the
    mountain first shines
it releases the down of a bird
from rock:

— Oh. We'll climb to the top!
— I'll wait at the foot.

— Of course we'll go up the mountain!
— I won't go up the mountain.

— And you'd admit you were here and didn't go
    up?

— I would. After all I did stand here.

Soon it will be light. Come on
let's go up!
— Forget the mountain! There's nothing
there. Nothing. Except what
cannot be reached
in the light

## UNPRONOUNCED VOWELS

Blue
the blue of the sky won't be bluer than this

clear
the screen of the mountains of Moab no clearer
    than this

the horizon is not drawn
with hieroglyphics but with unpronounced
    vowels.

With names they come
a fleet of names rowing toward you with the
    long oars

of slave ships.

And you go up like someone escaping. Call,
the gate is transparent
and locked. Even if you burst in and tear her
    veils

she is still hidden from you:

all my shores flooding. And more
than can be expressed in all the vowels.

## NO END OR BEGINNING

Stone over stone between stones.
The fire.
The drums.
The treason.
When all is silenced when all is dead by His
command
and alive
in a light that won't be destroyed
light to light between lights

— will not die!
Will live enslaved. It's not a mistake. No,
no crown for kings
— slavery. Take it! Or
get out

## LADDER

3,000 stairs to St. Catherine's
(they say it's more)
3,000 days the serfs of the mountain carved
(they say it's more)
so that St. Catherine's would be laddered in
 stone
to the mountain of mountains —
As you go down the last thousand
the monastery closes over you and a voice
from the wall comes back to you
in golden bells:

## ALL MY BELLS

The trembling day. The glory of my holy men in
black!
The bitter valley lies at our feet
because your dream will never pierce
the mountain. Forgive them Our Father
forever.
They never understood
what Jacob's ladder was made of.

## TWELFTH GATE:

## A FAREWELL SONG AND WORDS FROM THE DRUNK WHO EMBRACES AN EMPTY BOTTLE LIKE A GUITAR

The best woman, young man,
is a desired woman. The best way, my friend,
leads to a sea to a desert
to an odor of salt and rain an odor of stone
        scorched by the sun
a taste of ore of iron and blood
to a place from which there is no way
except for the ones who go.

Be thirsty, brother,
be thirsty. Only the one who is thirsty
has enough

and more than enough.

## IT'S LATE

Naked soil is the way to my beloved.
I come to her like someone coming to a tryst.
I quietly try to rebuild
a city, transparent. To sail confused houses
in two-way streets. To give them back
their faces, to arrange
rotating crops, to let the sea
break through into the small square
rooms and wash the frost flowers
and sand stripes alternately from the windows
like an old-fashioned devoted servant. Already

there is a road.
A road sign.
It's really possible to go. I will only hang
my hat to sway
on the acacia branch. I will mount
the new streetlights in my eyes so they won't
close
in difficult moments. On the neck of the weather
vane

I have already fastened my tie
with the pure gold pin
I inherited from my father. I will spread

my shirt before the first policeman's
dog who comes on time
running in front of his master. And my shoes
I will leave my shoes —
for the cat
until a better story is found
for the city children
and you
only you, my little sister, will I take with me
on my back. To carry you beyond
my naked plot of soil.

## from
## OBSERVATIONS

(*Tatzpiot*)
1977

. . . she is also before you: Here I am
Let me go please let me

## AND HOW THEY RISE

And how they rise . . . surround   come near
    flinch
and stay in the curtain. And I, as you know,
have nothing but one white page.

And how they swarm. With gaping mouths they
    tremble
on a narrow pier. This is not land, I say,
brothers. And all, all of them are here, and how
    they

just are. The shoemaker and the wagoner
and the tailor, even the singing tailor.
Only their heads are exchanged. Their nails dig
deep in my side. And they break out of the sea.

While my hand still sways over my eyes, they
    demand:
if you weren't cast up as the land for our sakes
who's the ark for? And you —

and how they stare. There's no sea,

I say to them, brothers — no
ship in my hands. No sign on my forehead.

Ghosts, you cursed ones, leave me alone!

And how they submit. The whip in front of
the shoemaker in front of the wagoner the feed
    bag
and the tailor the singing tailor
wrapped in seaweed and salt

she is also before you: Here I am.
Let me go please let me

## OBSERVATION AT DAWN

The night is still silky. Curtains are drawn
from the edge of the dream in a slow rhythm.
Red silk. We are both awake
trying quietly to spin the thread
cut off between the ribs. I'm reluctant
to look at this rain
beating at the windows.

And inside the night
is still silky. Your breath a soft thicket
guarding the border. When I count
the number of pulse beats, as if not believing,
and find signs in them, suddenly my eyes
discover my body, my arms stretched
over the sheet, lying there
naked (I must get them back somehow).

Rain
it's just rain! Like an oath I repeat
for the third time. Not your blood.
Then my finger taps on your throat
groping like a blind man's cane.

## OBSERVATION AT THE END OF A JOURNEY

I wanted to be born at the farthest limit of the
    world.
I'll explore it, I told myself,
biting big chunks of it.
And when I want, I'll go
straight to the core.
That's the way of the world I thought in my
    innocence,
around and around the parings
until I know what it tastes like.

And you were within me. Seven times more
    clear
than the light of my eyes.
Do you find me an absolute fool
if, at the opening of an unknown field,
with a butterfly net in my hand,
I still kneel
in front of insects and grasshoppers.

## ON THE WAY

Mother and father are beginning to die inside
    me.
Thirty years after their deaths in the storm
they withdraw quietly from my rooms,
from my moments of grace.

I'm sure about it. Voices and words have
    stopped,
they're free now. They no longer visit
my house, but not because they are angry.
A living man must be on his own.

Somewhere father is getting up early,
walking around in his sandals, pretending
as usual he doesn't see how mother cries
as she knits a warm sweater for her son,
camped on the way in the night.

## OBSERVATION ON JERUSALEM AT TWILIGHT AND A DIALOGUE

When did flocks leave the streets of Jerusalem?
We got up at dawn
and there weren't any flocks in the streets of
    Jerusalem.

When were wolves silent through the nights of
    Jerusalem?
That night we woke
and the desert withdrew from the edge of
    Jerusalem.

When did the camel trains quit the streets of
    Jerusalem?
Yesterday an old man died
who saw camels led through the squares of
    Jerusalem.

And mad dogs? Are there any still in Jerusalem?
I saw a covered well, and there's the new moon.
Why shouldn't there be mad dogs in Jerusalem?

And how does a man die in Jerusalem? When his
time comes.
Each man earns his death
though men fall in flocks in the hills of
Jerusalem.

And when is nothing brighter than Jerusalem?
When people who live there say to each other:
Let's go home and turn on the light.

## THERE'S NO ONE WITHOUT A CLOCK

There's no one without an alarm clock
on the table
or in the blood. After the defeat
I entered my room and closed myself in.
Until I had made up my mind
I did not bolt the door.
When I'd made up my mind
I could not force myself to lock up
my house, and bolt the door.

A strange fragrance burst from the city
chained in its twilight, when the clock
crazily rang. My daughter!
I expected the door to open — but the clock
like a bird call, strong without meaning,
rings
and rings
— doesn't anyone hear it but me?

## I DON'T KNOW IF MOUNT ZION

1

I don't know if Mount Zion would recognize
itself
at midnight in the fluorescent light
when there's nothing left of Jerusalem
but its beauty
wakeful in the milky light that glides
over its limbs   still wings
lift it from the sunken desert slowly
higher than the stars
this strange shell that floats out of the night
transparent giant
so much sky
washes over it
I don't know if Mount Zion looks into my heart
holding its breath now in pain and pleasure
behind a barred window
and who is it meant for
at midnight

2

These olive trees that never knelt
their knowledge hidden
their wrinkles carved this whole blue fan
on the road of the Hinnom Valley
I don't know if Mount Zion sees the things
that have changed our image
out of all recognition. Hands that touched it
every day like a mother's
touching the forehead of her son
sank dropping into the sleep
of the Dead Sea —
does it hear the cry
from the market of the gates
or the rush of my prayer from the shadow —
what's the use of friends who watch from the
        galleries
while our hearts struggle in the arena
and what's the sense of poets if we don't
know how to ask

Mount Zion    does it really exist
or is it like our love that glows from another
        light
rising
night after night

# ECCLESIASTES, RABBI IBN EZRA AND ZIMMEL THE BEGGAR

1

I hated life, said Ecclesiastes. And Rabbi
    Abraham
Ibn Ezra said *life* in the holy tongue is plural,
*hai-yim*, for all of us
*living* today. And there's *life, hai-yim*,
as in death and *life* — nothing
singular about that either.
                    So much for Reb Abraham.
There's also a kind of irregular life
with a future in spite of its past.
But when the sounds and syllables break
— *hai* — *ha* — *ha* — under stress,
linguists, grammarians give up,
experts can't open their mouths.
At this point we see

2

Zimmel the beggar,
both legs crippled.

Scene 1    Stands amazed.

Scene 2    Stands amazed.
Scene 3    Still stands (and how explain
a man who sits on stumps?) and begs
in the square that's changed. When suddenly
he feels the future in his cut-off legs
what's clearly    decided
that he will be only
a name    unknown
and no one will get out of there    alive.

3

So he stands. Begging as he always does
a minute, no more.
His crotch covered in rags,
his pants rolled up under his sad belly
(those two legs went
in the Czar's war), Zimmel the beggar
flees by the skin of his teeth, his hands,
up the drainpipe
to the sixth floor.

4

People. Down
there in the cobbled street,

and all of them wise as they try to decide
if escape is heroic
in the plural. While Zimmel the beggar's
outstretched
hands seize the one drainpipe.
He hangs there and dangles,
blood in his sweat. Foul breath. And the people
see
thunder: from the gate to the fence
everyone and the world still
alive.

5

A shout. Zimmel's up there! Our Zimmel's gone
mad!
He climbs with his hands and he shoves
his fat body through the crack
between beams of the roof and beams of the
world
and he smells the fabulous
stuffed can of garbage ready for his hideout
in the attic of the highest house in the Jews'
Street.

Now Zimmel the man will be sanctified and
glorified
for nine months as though for eternity.

And shouts from the fishmarket. Zimmel, come
down!
He'll ruin us, I swear! How can you
stand such a sight! They with their masses of feet
and he with the fear of his stumps.
Tucking his cut-off limbs under his belly,
Zimmel as monkey
at the farthest edge of the wall
on the sixth floor
stares down at them. He sticks out his tongue
and speaks to the frenzied town: I
*Ha-ha-ha-i i*
LIVE . . .

6

Some time later. Not one of those people
is around. Only a wooden cock
scorched on the roof, and Zimmel,
turning his head
like a weathervane in a ghost town,

rolling down the smoking stairs,
a bundle of rags. From the sixth floor
Zimmel swings his strapped body
toward what yesterday
was a city.
Wait a minute! Stunned, Zimmel finds
his left arm begging as it always has
in the empty square
of tomorrow's town.

7

For fifty good years you never
cried. Who'll listen now.

What used to be the Jews' Street heard
Zimmel cry
that morning. Broken sounds of his voice
fall and rise, crying and laughing:
*hai-hai-hai-*
*yim*! LIFE.
Against something spelled out.
Only in the plural, it leans to the past
and perhaps to the future. Suddenly
Zimmel the beggar

strikes his stumps with a terrible blow.
He says Zimmel, *mein kind*
let's start from the beginning.

## FORBIDDEN OBSERVATION

They get up from their mourning early on the
  eighth day, released,
wipe their foreheads with the backs
of their hands, uncover the mirrors,
touch the light.

The violin tuner tightens four strings
for them. Heads to the side
they test the sound
with their thumbs.

Continue the melody where
it was interrupted. Without a false note.
Because they forget for the moment
their mechanical prayers.

If there is a listener who truly listens,
they'll find their freedom
in the core of his silence.

## THIS WAY, THIS WAY

You are the mother of my lost children some in
the fire some
in the forest some waiting for a gate that did not
open you are the mother of my beautiful unborn
children for their sake I followed you
to the ends of invention
a land not sown
has no
end

from
TO

(*El*)
1980

The pain passes as it comes.
Often
there's nothing in its place.

TO MYSELF

Mathematicians take a huge area like a whole
world
and divide it into smaller areas, identical,
smaller than the eye can see.
Parts so exact don't need
an empty space between them.
Mathematicians
do it with only three forms:
isosceles triangle, square,
and hexagon, reliable instruments,
of course. My fear taught me
to try something else: when I could no longer
bear
the space surrounding me, I wanted to manage
something smaller
like a cell, dividing itself
without fission. Not looking for answers
to every question. Only to discover what is
nagging me. Still trying: forty years
and more. Why did I want to get rid
of that hidden fear?
After all, if I fall dead in the empty space
it's not the mathematicians who'll be surprised.

## POTATO PIE

1

The father wore an overcoat with a narrow
velvet collar.

2

Once in a while there was a striped suit
underneath and a shirt,
always neatly pressed.

3

Sorrow already on his clothes
like an eternal crease.

4

There was no radio at home. And no end to his
curiosity,
his thoughts awake at night walking
everywhere.

5

In his time he figured out correctly
the results of the Russo-Japanese War, a bit late.

6

He liked potato pie with salt herring.

7

When he couldn't have herring he made do
with the brine.

8

Suddenly the first World War
was over. A year later
Poland's liberation began. In 1919
he inherited a stone building

9

in the capital. On the bank of the river, with 22
condemned apartments. When he was already
a landlord, with tenants

10

and creditors

11

he still loved the potato pie his wife
made in all seasons.

12

They loved the sea
because another country came close
reflected in its waters.

13

He dreamed he'd go back

14

. . . . . . . . . . . . . . . . . . . . . . . . . . . . . .

15

So he went back. The day he imagined
his father returned
he lost his voice. And more.

16

He stood on the threshold.

17

There was no witness to see
the father
still standing on the threshold

18

not remembering the time. How long
his mouth was wide open

19

                                        and silent.
Until he moved his lips. Until his tongue
began to work, until his voice was back
and the echo
                    the father

20

behind the muslin curtain and the boy,
a buzzing in his head.

21

From that time on he feels a buzzing
in his head. Like pieces of a heart scraping his
    temples
and not only when

22

                                        there's an uninvited guest,
present without having come. Or

when he plays with his grandson: all the colors
        of the rainbow
in a soap bubble ready to burst
on the window screen.
                                        Then
it's there — this buzzing in his head!

23

The pain passes as it comes.
Often
there's nothing in its place.

## AND THERE YOU WERE

*in memory of Zivia Lubetkin*

And there you were next to
the TV in a tightly packed circle,
everyone watching, following
a small research submarine
sunk at the bottom of the sea.
Tense the way you are.

It was a well-done documentary
about people in distress.
On the small screen
two experienced sailors
were trapped in the depths,
their radio out of order.

We saw the ships. Summoned from Scotland.
And over a vast expanse of sea
fast ships, huge planes rushed
from Canada with the latest rescue equipment,
the whole great effort
for the sake of two young men
on the verge of despair.

You held your breath. I saw you were moved
like us
by the courage of those boys
in a terrible test of endurance.
Until they were saved.
And I nearly made a fool of myself
saying: Hey! What's the matter —
why all the fuss? I knew someone,
a frail girl, who was deep
in an ocean — not pacific at all, not the
Atlantic,
sunk for seven years without
a wireless. Without any radio without a single
connection to the air
outside.

Ships moved above her without
stopping
huge planes travelled without the slightest
change of course.
She called from the depths.
They heard her wrestling with the elements
black
red
blue

struggling for oxygen. For a last breath. Until
the boy came. We know him,
that boy who came from the end of the shaft

to lead her hand in hand blinded by gas
to the exit from Warsaw's sewer.
Luckily it was only half streaming
with excrement. And on to some refuge.

Now Kazik is also glued to the TV
in Baka, Jerusalem, watching astonished
how in a superb performance (the English, those
        English!)
they play back minute by minute the hours of
        distress
of people whose distress can be played back.
His old dog scratches itself at his feet
and he sits after a long day managing the
        supermarket,
dislocated in the soft armchair, his eyes closed.
Boy of the sewers. Looking towards
where you pass now like an atmospheric
        disturbance
between the communications satellite and the
        North Star.

## CHANGING THE ORDER

1

Finished his shower. With the blade of a
squeegee
my neighbor scrapes what's left of the water to
the mouth
of the drain. It's not my neighbor's fault the
drain
is clogged. Not my neighbor's fault that
sometimes
a drowning voice comes from the drain.

Now he rubs himself dry. In a minute
he'll switch off the lights
according to plan: toilet     kitchen     porch
and the fluorescent light over the purple sofa
and over the Degas. Still bound by the rules
from the days of the country's recession,
he'll switch off all the lights. Then he'll turn on
the small night lamp, set the TV
at the lowest possible volume
and in tan bedroom slippers walk to his armchair
one step at a time
so as not to disturb his shadow.

2

If I were my neighbor
I'd change the order:            first turn on the TV.
                                        Then switch on
                          the night lamp and switch on
                   the fluorescent light and switch on
                          the porch light and switch on
        the one in the toilet + kitchen + living-room
                                        and switch on
all available light in all the rooms and leave
every light on and get into the shower.
And without taking my clothes off open
the shower spray and stand tall under
the cold stream and sing

sing like I used to
ever since I grew up
with my off-pitch voice
singing and lathering
lathering and singing
till I run out of the songs of my childhood.

# UNCOLLECTED

And behind all this, my love,
aren't you
still hiding?

## LAST STORM

*in memory of Yohevet Bat-Miriam*

1

The storm, the last
in my life, won't come again
I know

in your open arms.
With closed eyes I grope for
you in the darkness
I know

I have made. And the shadows
don't fade by themselves.
Images. Memories —

when I add them to what is already
under the bed
the night sweeps more.

The last
storm. There won't be another like it
in my life, I know.

2

Sometimes,
you understand, it seems
that nothing is here
and never was.

Sometimes
(don't say it!)
I'm already there.

And the pride of a fallen man
is only the pride of a man
robbed
and rising like someone who's beaten.
He stumbles,
hanging on to a ledge, and he
walks on the walls
back where he came from,

moves on the stones
that were there before
the great clearing of stones. Maybe
frogs were left underneath,
and the tongue of the swamp below
the lawns we had nurtured.

Now I must find a witness
for our lives
— do you understand? A man needs proof
he was
here. Yes here. And
the place is still his. The trees
and the burnt offering.

Look! You come out from behind
the white stone. Call —
I return and step over the threshold.

3

When I asked my soul to die
in sickness, isolation,
in a hopeless war;
when I asked my soul to die
what did not stop flowing
in my shrinking veins was
you and
you.
You.

In a thousand reflections, my love,
I atone for you.

4

Now I know why
our house is concrete and why
we wear jeans and why
Jerusalem is united. Why we want
a different theater. And why
we need a crosswalk
and a traffic signal,
the flash of authority.
And why clever members of parliament
are absent from the plenum
in permanent rotation,
and why I read the morning news
and the late news
compulsively
but for God's sake, why
do I not stop talking
to you!
To you —

So many days
with no answer, with no
certainty.
When and why

do you keep quiet?

5

Someone who is free can
get up and leave,
and someone who is free cannot
get up and leave.

For who knows
the ones who will really judge us?
Or how many words
we've wasted:
they don't build roads in the wilderness
or bridges between nations —

our fine loves
were not wrapped up at the butcher's
in the weekend literary supplements.

6

I did not bring you plastic flowers
that never wilt.
We already paid the full price,
even for the last

bouquet. I never imagined
I would cry in rhyme.

7

A footnote: placed — by chance? — in the file
and written on guard duty near the cow shed
of the kibbutz.

Calves are blind for one day
when they're born. Then they get up, drink milk
from a bottle, and see whatever can be seen
through the eyes of an innocent calf.
They say ma-a-a
to the world.

And Jews die blind
from too much seeing
the world as it was
and as it will be.

8

We'll lose in the end, my daughter,
I know.

9

When I go
I'll go. I'll take
nothing with me
on my star travels
except an unpublished
poem and you.

10

And the fragrance
of my grandchild tugging at my hair.
And my unfinished homeland:
(daughter)
(daughter)
— in the end we'll
lose?

## FALLING ROCKS

1

When I first saw the sea
the sea was
the sea, the surrounding mountains
only mountains,
my mother beside me
and I, let's assume,
without guilt.

2

And the sun covered the full face
of the sea.
If I'd been older, eight
maybe nine, when you have the right
to a watch of your own
and can read the time without help,
I'd have held it up
on my wrist
and looked at it then and known
for sure
that

3

in the Crimea the local time is now
3:45 just before dawn
the last summer before the Great War.
Sh h h . . .

Above the white terrace
in a minute
His Highness himself
will appear at the royal window
to watch the sunrise.
Sh h h!

4

The gulls whispered,
the waves whispered, my Aunt Fanya
whispered: quarter of an hour, less
than a quarter of an hour.

5

Aunt Fayna has opened her parasol
for the third time (3:45 before the sunrise!)
and while she swings it above her feverish head
for no reason

bobbing back and forth
like the beak of a fluttering swan —
she looks up there
her lips parted

6

and the people
from Odessa and Kherson, from Moscow and St.
Petersburg
who gathered at dusk under sheets and mosquito
netting
and blazing Samarkand scarves
are still asleep
stretched out wherever they can
on the pitted cliff
a wall of rock
facing Bydarskiya Vorota
and the Black Sea

7

and when here and there
a vague buzzing is heard, someone turns over
on his stung side or rises

like a huge bat
out of the pages of a book

8

                    this is the kind of thing
one never forgets, says my Aunt Fanya,
and just to me: Dearie!
Don't fall asleep. You mustn't miss THIS!
And my mother (my head on her breast) doesn't
    call me
by name, but you'd have to be an idiot
not to understand it's not for the sake of
    argument
she seems to be telling my aunt
that's not what's important (Aunt Fanya her eyes
    still
fixed on the shadow of the terrace behind us any
    minute
the Czar is supposed to appear like any other
    spectator
there with his whole blonde retinue
and clearly Aunt Fanya can't stand
the suspense), and that's why
the warm hand of my mother turns my face

away from the white marble of the palace
down towards the inner darkness.

9

She points her finger.
There. The skin of the Black Sea
will crack in a minute.

10

I watch this instructing
finger.

11

In this one place, the sun,
mother whispers against my forehead,
will come out like a bridegroom
to welcome his bride
and we'll see, whispers mother, an incredible
wonder like nothing in nature,
the whole world held
in an enormous flame
land — sea — sky —
will be one.

Without fires, without blood,
without terror.

12

As if it broke out of the depths
I heard it
                    the sun
had risen. I couldn't imagine a bridegroom
meeting his bride.
But as soon as the edge of the sea
turned pink
like roses opening,
and a marvelous crimson suddenly flooded
the base of the rock

13

                                        below me —
was it simply the instinct of a child
unaware of danger
or the beginning of curiosity
that would never be satisfied

14

— above me I saw my mother
pulling at her hair.

15

I see her hair
thrown in a lime pit later
ends gilded by flames of the sunrise
and I think of the hair of my mother
in Bydarskiya Vorota
like the burning bush —
something that rare
— how she stood there screaming

16

They rescued me, pulled me
up to her on a rope. Mother!
Nothing happened, I wanted . . .
But no one believed
I just wanted to get close enough to see
if the Black Sea was really red.

17

I forgave her
though my bottom trembled under her hard
hand,
and even now I know
she was crazy with fear —

all for the drowning I didn't drown!

DANGER: FALLING ROCKS
But I didn't know how to read
the Cyrillic letters yet. To read at all.
On such a night with everyone so wound up
waiting for the great magic
who could tell a warning sign
from WELCOME
TO BYDARSKIYA VOROTA

18

I watch from the distance. Something
like a rope stretched
in the air.
For everything forbidden,
for whatever's taboo, I've only been warned
after the event.

19

And if I weren't innocent
would I have cried? Finding only the Black Sea
in my small palm — water.
Not red. Not black.

Oily
and salty.

20

Another time we came to the sea
almost by accident. Far away from the city
far from our friends or anyone
else. It was the last day
of summer before World War II.
We walked along the shore searching
for contradictions:
                                        to find ourselves
and not be afraid of finding.
The bed of the North Sea was incredibly naked
next to the embankment. Quick
in a crazy abandon
we tore off our clothes
and plunged into it.
And the sea was no longer
only a sea.
The mountains around us seemed more
than just mountains.
The line of the great horizon, the soft contours
were there only to cover

you and me.

21

And there was a third time

22

  No! It's not important
to be exact. Whether it happened on the shore
of the Aegean or where we hid ourselves
on the beach at Marseilles:
you, my love, were there behind me,
Mother was behind me,
Aunt Fanya with her funny parasol,
my brother, all the others.
I could have said to them: Right, dress!
I could have said: Attention!
Just by a sign. For I heard them behind my back
out of the cresting waves
a whole continent.
                    And the sea — how can I say this —
turned into a crosswalk
for the ones who carry a burning stone in their
    hearts
for the ones who go down to the depths of the
    ocean with us

for the ones who walk behind us —
a sea made dry.

23

My digital watch (with a winder,
timer, alarm bell) flashes
5:45 p.m.
I go back.
Young pine trees. The geraniums beautiful
        always
                                                        ferns
                                                used condoms
                                                    wrappers
                                cartons of chocolate milk.
A barbed wire fence. Clean gravel
under it. I see a cafe, white chairs, tennis courts
and next to the showers — 1 2 3 —
tiled terraces    red yellow black yellow red
I look at the sea, the sky
still stainless
blue.

24

And when you did not come to me out of the
        empty space
but in the shape of a single surfboard
with a boy in black rubber
rising and sinking
sinking and rising
a quivering sail in his hand —
I couldn't hang on.

Till I noticed a faded sign.
And why wasn't Hebrew enough
to warn us of the danger of falling rocks?
It was in English: FALLING ROCKS.
So why not warn the French in their language:
DANGER D'ÉBOULEMENT
or Spaniards who lose their way:
PELIGRO DE DERRUMBAMIENTO
and what about Arabic:
خطر انهيار                    I try to recall
if I ever saw a sign like that
in my mother tongue.

25

Yiddish for this
would be useless now.

26

The sun moves south of Netanya
with a strong tilt toward the sea.
From here I can guess exactly where
it will dip under,
the radius of the brightness
that will spread out as it sets.
It's dark now. The sea runs in,
runs out. Listen.
Above me the sky of a summer night
(the seventh war is over)
and already three stars. Smells and smoke
from the barbecue.
                                        I go back
and look, stopped by what's at my feet,
rinds with the insides eaten away,
empty cigarette cartons,
all the torn paper not
swept into garbage carts
by the brooms of the national parks.

I look, amazed at what's distant,
the softness and ease of the waves
rocking in the twilight, desire
that echoes from the long reach of time
on the tense path
                                        as in the air
through which I go back now
and the view of the orange groves covered
by the last light on the horizon.
And behind all this, my love,
aren't you
still hiding?

# NOTES

## I. FROM ALL THE LOVES

"They Build Houses in Ein Hahoresh"
p. 27 *Ein Hahoresh*

Literally "Spring of the Plowman," the name of the kibbutz in the Sharon Plain where Abba Kovner has made his home since 1946.

"Lord of Hosts"
p. 33 *ribbon*

It would be impossible to document all the personal and historical allusions in Kovner's poems, but perhaps one will suffice. The sister-daughter with ribbons in her braids appears many times in Kovner's work, as a symbol for all the lost, murdered, unborn victims. In a speech Kovner made in Italy in 1945 to survivors and refugees and members of the Jewish Brigade who had come to rescue them, he said:

> . . . for a long time the Jews (whom the Nazis had already confined to walled ghettos and begun to slaughter) refused to believe that these people were capable of throwing grenades at the naked bodies of young girls, that they were capable of practising their marksmanship on the sexual organs of live women, and that one day they would suddenly lure 400 Jewish children, order their mothers to dress them in their clean holiday clothes and put ribbons, expressly, ribbons in their braids in order to bring them before a medical board, and then tens of doctors in white coats would take the skin off their living faces in order to graft the delicate skin of Jewish children onto bodies of German soldiers with severe burns.

"Near"

p. 34 *heaps of feathers*

During a pogrom, the attackers would tear pillows open looking for gold and money. After such assaults, the air was filled with feathers in Jewish villages.

"Everyone Who Comes"

p. 39 *Eliahu, the Gaon of Vilna*

*Gaon* is the title used for oustanding Talmudic scholars. Elijah (Eliahu) ben Solomon, 1720–1797, was revered as the greatest Talmudic authority of his time.

II. MY LITTLE SISTER

Kovner has said, "When I wrote *My Little Sister*, I charged it with what were perhaps my most intimate associations to the experience of the Holocaust, and yet it became the poem best understood by my readers. I myself did not understand everything I was trying to say . . . It was much more to me than the testimony of a victim, than an individual tragedy. In the little sister's endless expectation of redemption, in contrast to the realized world of the Dominican 'Sisters,' in the secret way in which the child absorbs and learns the facts of life, in the web of illusion she spins around herself, and finally, in the wish to remember what has not yet happened, or to put it another way, in the dread of what is to come — there is something which seems to transcend personal tragedy and historical event, something which perhaps is at the very center of our experience as Jews and human beings." *On the Narrow Bridge* (Tel Aviv: Sifriat Poalim, 1981), p. 184.

p. 65

*Oh You who commanded us* . . .

A fragmentary echo of the traditional benediction recited before carrying out a divine commandment.

p. 67

The *hallah*, or twisted loaf of Sabbath bread, was part of the festive wedding meal along with chicken soup.

p. 75

*behold you/are consecrated.*

Part of the formula recited by the groom to the bride during the marriage ceremony: "Behold you are consecrated unto me with this ring according to the law of Moses and Israel." The previous line also alluded to a wedding, being a verbatim quotation from Song of Songs 8:8, the verse that introduces the little sister who is to be married.

p. 76

*Behold you —*

The truncated beginning of the marriage ceremony formula, made clear by the allusion in the third line to the traditional bridal canopy under which the ceremony is conducted.

p. 78

The Hebrew here imitates the peculiar style of the medieval *piyut*, or liturgical poem, with its exaggerated use of internal rhyme, alliteration, wordplay, and its densely allusive quality. The key allusion here, made clear in the Hebrew through the insistence on the word *dodi*, "my love," is to the Song of Songs. In this section the translation has concentrated more on retaining the songlike quality than on the exact literal meaning.

p. 82

*a candle for the saving of her soul*

An allusion to the traditional Jewish practice in which the mourner, during the first week of bereavement or on the anniversary of a death, lights a candle for the "saving" or ascent of the departed soul.

p. 84

*Imi/imi.* Hebrew: "my mother, my mother," echoing the "with me" (*imi*) of the previous line. The repeated syllables may be, among other things, a counterpoint to an expected, "*And say with me/* amen/ amen."

## III. A CANOPY IN THE DESERT

This book-length poem (*Hupa Bamidbar*) which followed *My Little Sister* is about a strange journey and a wedding which does not happen. The *hupa* is a wedding canopy, still used in Jewish marriages, to remind us of the tent ceremony in biblical times when the veiled bride was brought into the groom's tent (Gen. 24:67). The *midbar* is the desert where Moses led 600,000 Hebrew slaves out of Egypt. It is the desert at the foot of Mount Sinai where Moses made his Covenant with God, and it is the desert where the newly created state of Israel has fought three wars for its right to exist.

*A Canopy in the Desert* is divided into twelve *gates*, an archaic use of the Hebrew word *sha'ar*, which used to introduce books— a first page, a first chapter. Two *gates* are reprinted here:

*Eighth Gate*

Kovner's narrator-survivor-wanderer comes to Mount Sinai, the mountain of the giving of the Law. But between him and the mountain of God "There's nothing/ there. Nothing. Except what/ cannot be reached/ in the light." Another God stands in the shape of the monastery, and here again, as in *My Little Sister*, there is a dialogue between Christianity as realization and Judaism as expectation. It appears in the contrast between the 3,000 stone steps carved by the monks to the top of the mountain, and the metaphysical ladder of Israel which is Jacob's ladder ("All My Bells").

p. 87 *St. Catherine's Monastery.*

Located in the mountainous south central region of Sinai, this Greek Orthodox monastery, more than a thousand years old, is set at the base of Mount Sinai, believed to be the mountain where Moses received the Ten Commandments.

*The Mountain of Mountains.* A literal translation of the Hebrew name for Mount Sinai.

p. 89 *Unpronounced Vowels.*

The Hebrew title for this section is four Hebrew letters: *Alef, He, Vav, Yod.* These letters which are used today only as vowels and whose pronunciation has changed, had, in ancient times, a pronunciation of their own. They are referred to as "mothers of reading" in Hebrew, and the eleventh-century Spanish-Jewish poet Yehuda Halevi called them "mothers of the Torah and its roots." The poet hints here that these unclear kernels of the language are transmitted from as far as a lost planet. And they are filled with content and meaning, although we can no longer decipher them.

p. 91 *get out*

The Hebrew for "get out" is the untranslatable *lekh lekha*, "get thee out" in the King James translation of Gen. 12:1. In one of the best known passages in the Bible, God tells Abraham to leave his home and journey to the promised land. The history of Israel begins with these words. In Kovner's poem, if the people who came to the foot of Mount Sinai rejected the Law, they would have to "get out," go back to Egypt. The choice is between two very different kinds of slavery.

*Twelfth Gate*

The journey comes to an end with an attempt to return to life, to sanity, to the real world. But only the dead know their time runs out. In the real world, among the living, the wanderer still carries his little sister on his back.

## IV. OBSERVATIONS

p. 102 "On The Way"

As the note on *ribbon* in the poem "Lord of Hosts" points up Kovner's personal and historical allusion, so perhaps a note on the last line of "On The Way" may illustrate the entire problem of translating Biblical allusions. What are we to make of the last line where the last two words in the Hebrew seem to make no sense? *Ba-derech ba-malon.* Translated literally, according to modern Hebrew usage, we get "on the road in the hotel." But an Israeli, who studies the Hebrew Bible from the earliest grades in school — as history, religion, literature — will hear an echo after these words and suddenly recall their source in only one place in the Bible, a crucial passage, Exodus 4:24. The King James translation reads, "by the way in the inn . . ."; the new Jewish Publication Society version, "at a night encampment on the way . . ."

The scene is a night encampment where Moses has stopped on his way back to Egypt after God has commanded him to return and deliver his people from slavery. And the line in Exodus continues, " . . . the LORD met him, and sought to kill him." The language is so obscure, the Hebrew so elliptic, God's motive so unclear, that rabbis and scholars have commented on this line for hundreds of years with no agreement as to its meaning. What seems certain is that a threat to life is made during a journey.

The last line of Kovner's poem seems opaque, but if one catches the biblical allusion (perhaps impossible in English translation), and then goes outside the poem to the facts of the poet's life as we know them, perhaps we can get at its meaning. There seems to be a link between the situation of the reluctant Moses, persuaded by God to lead his people to freedom, and that of Kovner, whose leadership of the Partisans from the Vilna ghetto was thrust upon him when the Nazis threatened to liquidate the entire ghetto if the first Partisan leader was not turned over to them. Kovner was also chosen to lead his people — out of the ghetto to possible safety. For him the responsibility of assuming leadership of the ghetto fighters at the age of 24, and having others follow him, weighed even more heavily than the threat to life — as they "camped on the way" to rescue and survival during the long night of the Holocaust (the "storm" in line 2 of the poem). This is personal history. But the line clearly evokes more than that.

p. 109 "Ecclesiastes, Rabbi Ibn Ezra, and Zimmel the Beggar"

*Rabbi Ibn Ezra* (1089–1164), Spanish philosopher, poet, grammarian, astronomer, and physician.

## V. TO

p. 119 "Potato Pie"

The original title of this poem is "Alte Zachen," the Yiddish cry of Jewish peddlars as they buy and sell old cast-off clothing and household articles.

p. 124 "And There You Were"

In memory of *Zivia Lubetkin*

Dedication to one of the founders (1914–1978) of Kibbutz Lohamei ha-Getta'ot, a leader of the Warsaw ghetto uprising who escaped from the ghetto at the last moment through the sewers.

## VI. UNCOLLECTED

p. 131 "Last Storm"

*In memory of Yohevet Bat-Miriam*

Dedication to a Hebrew poet whose major work was written between the two world wars against the background of the Jewish tragedy of this period (1901–1979).

p. 138 "Falling Rocks"

*Bydarskiya Vorota*: A resort on the Black Sea near Sevastopol in the Crimea, USSR, where thousands of tourists come in midsummer to watch the dramatic spectacle of the sunrise. Czar Nicholas had his summer palace nearby.